My name is Jade
And my name is Cade

We're in the third grade
And we love every dog ever made

Some humans can be mean
Some say dogs are not clean
But we love when dogs are seen
We love dogs of every gene

It's up to us to take the lead
Let's learn from what we read
Show the world what dogs need
We love dogs of every breed

Some dogs have it hard
Some are always on guard
Stuck outside, in a yard
Others have been oh so scarred

Rescue. Adopt. Foster. Volunteer.

This is Memo and he is white
His first five years full of fright

He was forced by some to fight and bite
But he knew that just wasn't right

He was saved one day and saw the light
His future looking oh so bright
No more living a life of spite
Adopted finally, he got on his flight

This is Memo today in his furever home.
He was adopted by the best mom ever and now gets to have lots of treats, play with his human and fur siblings, and snore as loud as he'd like while he sleeps.

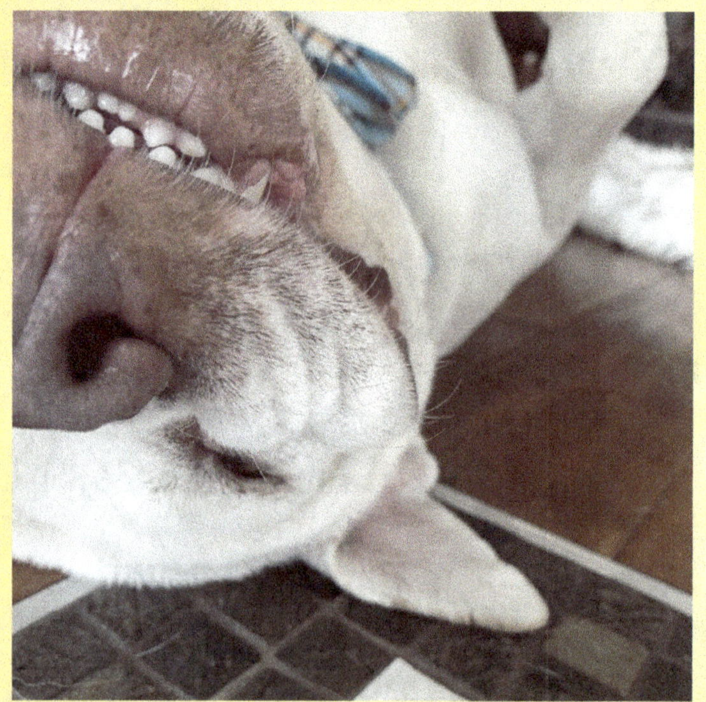

Say hi to Brindle B
She had a home, she thought maybe
But I guess her owner did not agree
He gave her away pretty much for free

She moved around from place to place
Hoping one day to find her space
To her furever home, she goes with grace
She meets her new mom with an embrace

This is Brindle today in her furever home. She was adopted by her paw-some mom and lives with her fur brother and sister. Brindle likes walks, butt scratches, and naps- and she LOVES car rides.

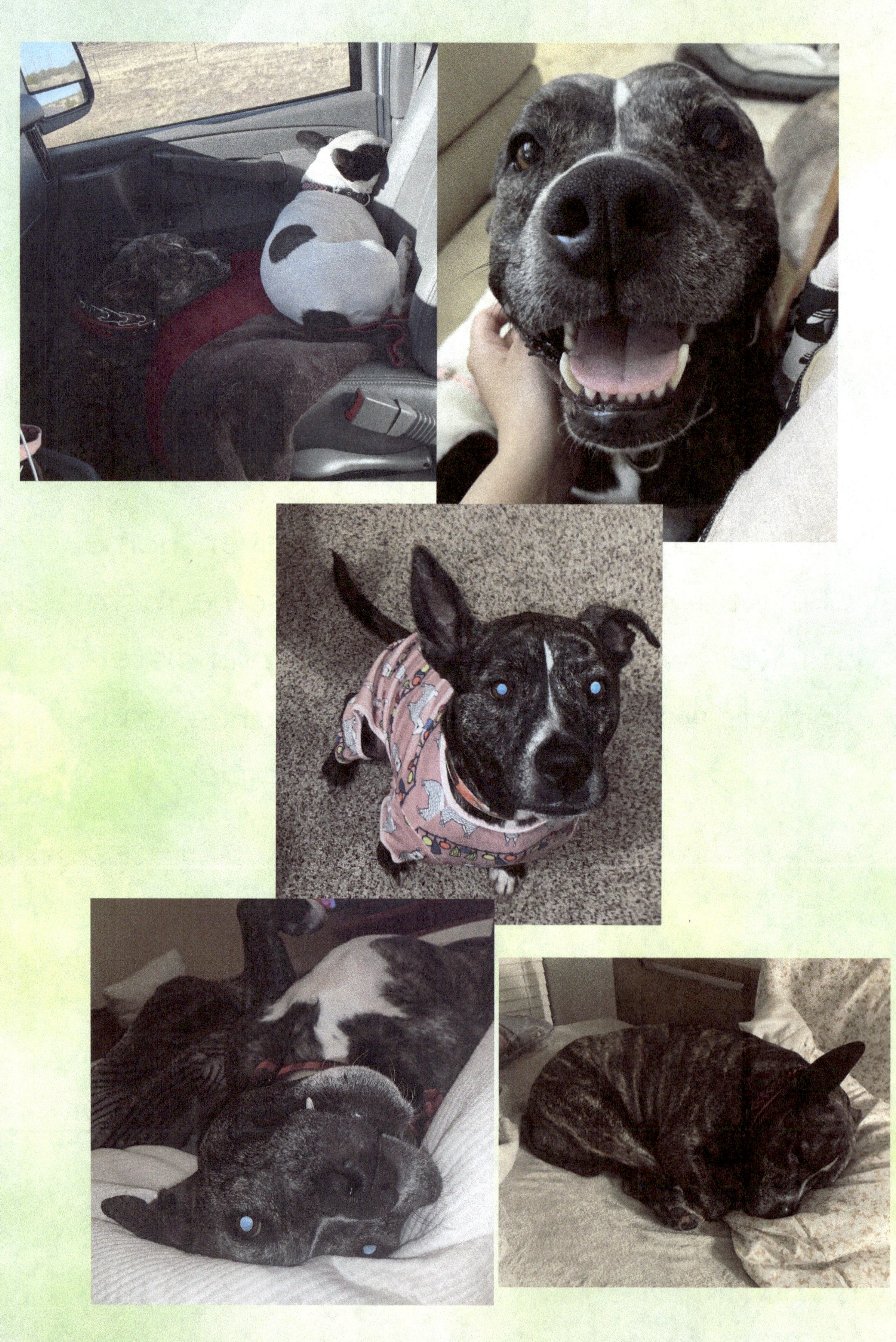

Benjamin was just a pup that day
When he was left out on the highway
Terrified of being a forever stray
Until a rescue found him and took him away

He lived with a foster for a little while
But she fell in love with him with a smile
Now they play and sleep and walk a mile
Years later creating a wonderful lifestyle

Today, Benjamin lives with his foster mom turned furever mom and his two fur sisters in sunny San Diego. He lives for cuddles, pets, and movie nights with mom.

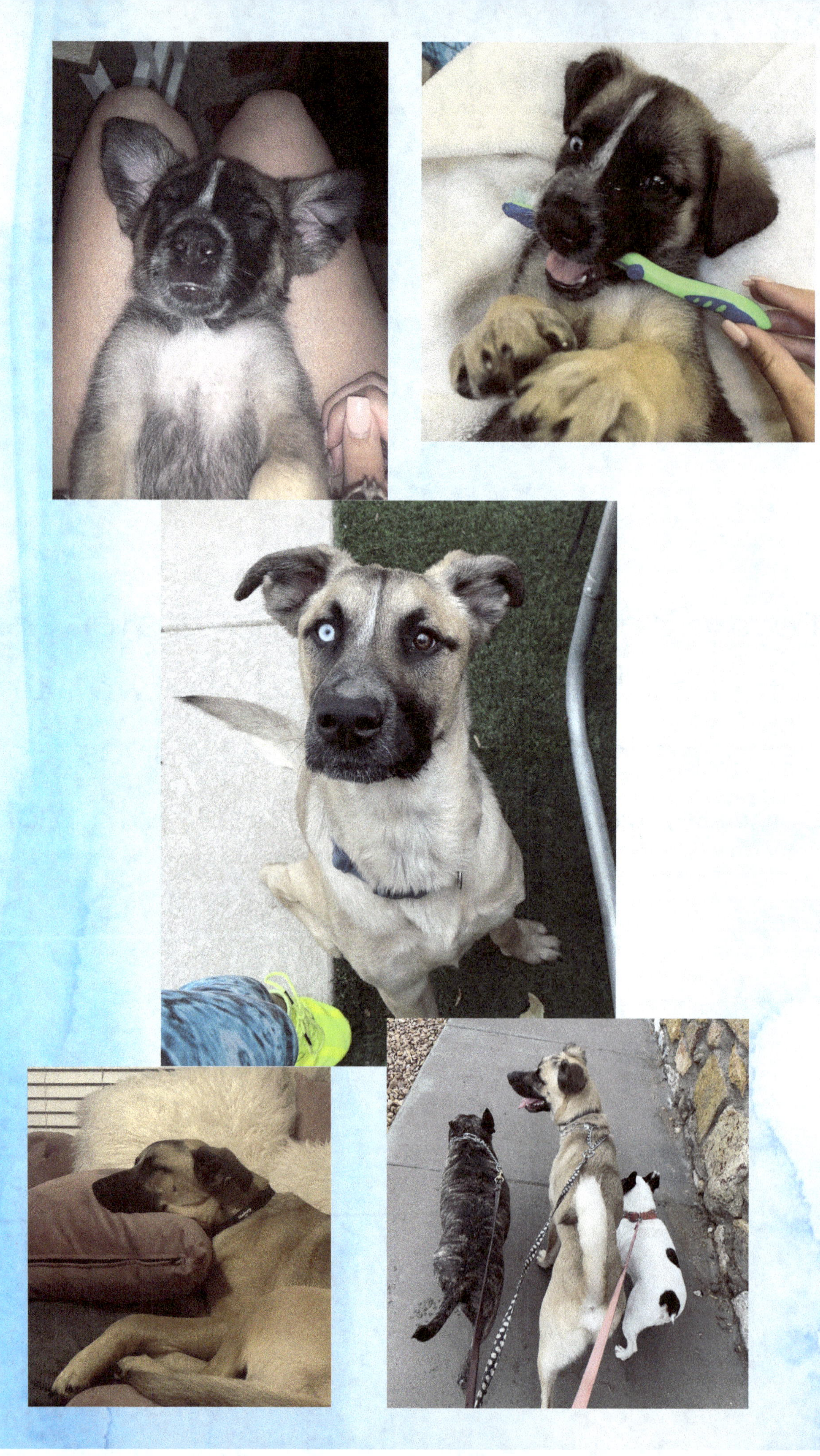

Milo was found with his mom and his sis
Out in the wild, we couldn't dismiss
The rescue found them, finally bliss
Next came a foster home with a big, big kiss

Milo's family came from afar
Loved him so much, they came by car
Now he's living like a star
Treats, dog parks, and walks so far

Milo now lives with his furever mom and his human and fur siblings. He loves his walks, playing, and going to doggy daycare!

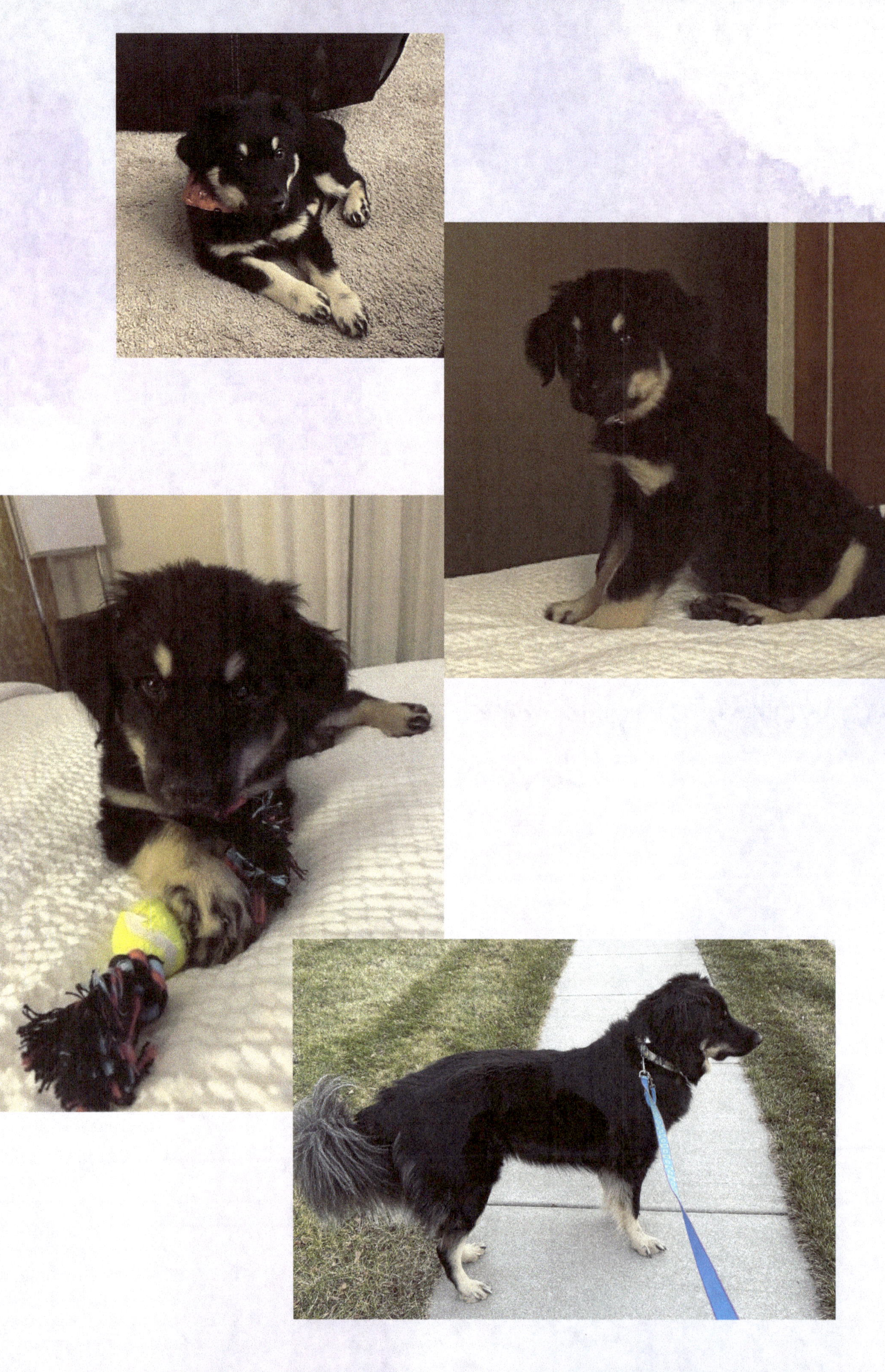

The End.

To find out how you can help dogs in your area, visit your local animal shelter, humane society, or non profit rescue.

Ways to help:

Donate. Donate food, blankets, collars/leashes, crates, beds, or money.

Volunteer. Help is always needed, volunteer to clean up stalls or to take dogs on walks.

Foster. See if you can become a foster. Dog food and vet bills are covered by the rescue, the dog just needs a warm home to stay in until they find their furever home.

Adopt. The best way to help is to adopt a dog. There are rescue groups for every breed of dog, and there are millions of dogs put to sleep each year due to overbreeding. Why not save a life instead of buying from a breeder?

www.ingramcontent.com/pod-product-compliance
Lightning Source LLC
Chambersburg PA
CBHW081922120726
47996CB00010B/3440